I0815376

DISCOVERING THE UNITED STATES

Minnesota

BY ARNOLD RINGSTAD

Kids Core

An Imprint of Abdo Publishing
abdobooks.com

abdobooks.com

Printed in China.
052024
092024

Cover Photo: Shutterstock Images
Interior Photos: Esperanza Casso/Shutterstock Images, 4–5; Rejean Aline Bedard/Shutterstock Images, 6 (top left); Michael P. Gadomski/Science Source, 6 (top right); Edgar Lee Espe/Shutterstock Images, 6 (bottom left); Piotr Wawrzyniuk/Shutterstock Images, 6 (bottom right); Dennis O'Hara/Shutterstock Images, 8; Sandrine Huet/Le Pictorium/Alamy, 10–11; Jack Kurtz/ZUMA Press, Inc./Alamy, 13; Stephen Maturen/Chicago Tribune/Tribune News Service/Getty Images, 14; Mayo Clinic/National Archives/PhotoQuest/Archive Photos/Getty Images, 16; Paul Brady Photography/Shutterstock Images, 18–19, 28 (Saint Paul); Jamie Eilat/Wikimedia Commons, 20; Shutterstock Images, 26; Sam Wagner/Shutterstock Images, 21, 28 (Duluth); Ken Wolter/Shutterstock Images, 22; AaronP/Bauer-Griffin/GC Images/Getty Images, 25; Red Line Editorial, 28 (map), 29

Editor: Laura Stickney
Series Designer: Katharine Hale

Library of Congress Control Number: 2023949347

Publisher's Cataloging-in-Publication Data

Names: Ringstad, Arnold, author.
Title: Minnesota / by Arnold Ringstad
Description: Minneapolis, Minnesota: Abdo Publishing, 2025 | Series: Discovering the United States | Includes online resources and index.
Identifiers: ISBN 9781098293932 (lib. bdg.) | ISBN 9798384913207 (ebook)
Subjects: LCSH: U.S. states--Juvenile literature. | Minnesota--History--Juvenile literature. | Midwest States--Juvenile literature. | Physical geography--United States--Juvenile literature.
Classification: DDC 973--dc23

All population data taken from:
"Estimates of Population by Sex, Race, and Hispanic Origin: April 1, 2020 to July 1, 2022." *US Census Bureau, Population Division,* June 2023, census.gov.

CONTENTS

CHAPTER 1
The Megamall 4

CHAPTER 2
The People of Minnesota 10

CHAPTER 3
Places in Minnesota 18

State Map 28
Glossary 30
Online Resources 31
Learn More 31
Index 32
About the Author 32

In 2023, the Mall of America had more than 500 stores. About 40 million people visit the mall every year.

CHAPTER 1

The Megamall

It was August 11, 1992. The country's largest shopping mall was about to open. At 9:25 a.m., shoppers in line counted down the last ten seconds. When the count reached zero, the doors opened. The shoppers stepped inside the Mall of America.

Minnesota Facts

DATE OF STATEHOOD
May 11, 1858

CAPITAL
Saint Paul

POPULATION
5,717,184

AREA
86,936 square miles (225,163 sq km)

STATE BIRD

Common loon

STATE TREE

Norway pine

STATE FLOWER

Showy lady's slipper

STATE FISH

Walleye

Each US state has a different population, size, and capital city. States also have state symbols.

This gigantic mall is in Bloomington, Minnesota. It made national news when it opened. The mall had more than 200 stores. Shoppers could take a break at its many restaurants. The mall even had an amusement park. About 150,000 people visited on opening day. The Mall of America remains a Minnesota icon.

Minnesota's Land

Minnesota is in the region of the United States known as the Midwest. The state borders Canada to the north. To the east of Minnesota is Wisconsin, and to the south is Iowa.

Counting Lakes

Counting a state's lakes can be difficult. The number depends on what is considered a lake. Minnesota has many small bodies of water. People often call these ponds instead of lakes. The state government estimates that Minnesota has 14,380 lakes.

Lake Superior is the largest of the Great Lakes. The Ojibwe people call it *gichigami*, or "great sea."

North Dakota and South Dakota are to the west. Minnesota's land includes forests, prairies, and hills. The state is home to animals such as wolves and common loons.

Minnesota is known as the Land of 10,000 Lakes. However, it actually has even more lakes than that. The state also borders Lake Superior in the northeast. Major rivers run through Minnesota too. These include the Mississippi River, Minnesota River, and Saint Croix River.

Minnesota's Climate

Minnesota has four seasons. The seasons have clear differences. Summers are hot and humid. In fall, the weather cools down. This season is often windy and rainy. Winter brings heavy snow and freezing temperatures. In spring, plants grow as the weather warms up. But snow can still fall as late as May.

Explore Online

Visit the website below. Does it give any new information about the Mall of America that wasn't in Chapter One?

Mall of America's Visitor Guide

abdocorelibrary.com/discovering-minnesota

Today, there are four federally recognized Dakota groups in Minnesota. They practice cultural traditions, such as dancing.

The People of Minnesota

The first people in Minnesota were American Indians. They have lived in the area for more than 12,000 years. By the 1600s, there were two major peoples living in what is now Minnesota. They were the Dakota and the Ojibwe nations.

At that time, the Dakota people moved with the seasons. They grew crops such as corn, beans, and wild rice. The Ojibwe traveled down rivers in birchbark canoes. They had times of war and peace with the Dakota.

Immigration

White settlers came to Minnesota in the early 1800s. They were mostly English, Scottish, and Irish. Other **immigrant** groups arrived in the

Welcoming Refugees

Minnesota has a history of welcoming **refugees**. Family and religious groups have supported these immigrants. The state government has helped them find housing. Politicians have also passed laws to aid these newcomers.

Minnesota has become a center for Hmong culture. At the Hmongtown Marketplace in Saint Paul, vendors sell traditional Hmong foods, fresh vegetables, and other goods.

late 1800s. These included Germans, Swedes, and Norwegians.

After the Vietnam War (1954–1975), many Hmong people from Laos came to Minnesota. The state now has the largest Hmong community in the nation. Immigrants from Somalia came in the 1990s. They were fleeing war and **famine** in their home country.

Dana Thompson, *left*, partnered with Chef Sean Sherman, *right*, to create Owamni. Menu items have included elk tacos, smoked bison, and wild rice.

Today Minnesota is about 83 percent white. It is 8 percent Black, 5 percent Asian, and 1 percent American Indian. About 6 percent of Minnesotans are Hispanic or Latino. The state's total population is about 5.7 million.

Culture

The cultures of Minnesota can be seen in its food. In 2021, Oglala Lakota chef Sean Sherman opened a restaurant in Minneapolis. The restaurant's ingredients are native to the area. These include bison, squash, and beans.

Swedish dishes such as meatballs are also popular in Minnesota. Hmong food is common too. One example is a soup dish called pho. Somali dishes include spicy curries and plates of meat.

Minnesota's culture can also be seen in sports. Since the state gets cold in winter, lakes and ponds freeze. Ice skating and hockey are popular activities. But football is the most popular sport to watch in the state.

The Mayo Clinic has a long history. Today, it serves more than 1 million patients every year and is a center for medical research. The clinic includes more than 30 buildings.

Industry

Farming is important in **rural** areas of Minnesota. Farmers grow corn, soybeans, and sugar beets. Cities have large **manufacturing** companies. General Mills makes food products. 3M creates products such as Post-it notes.

Health care is another big industry. The Mayo Clinic in Rochester is a world-famous hospital. Many Minnesotans work in the service industry. This includes workers in restaurants and stores.

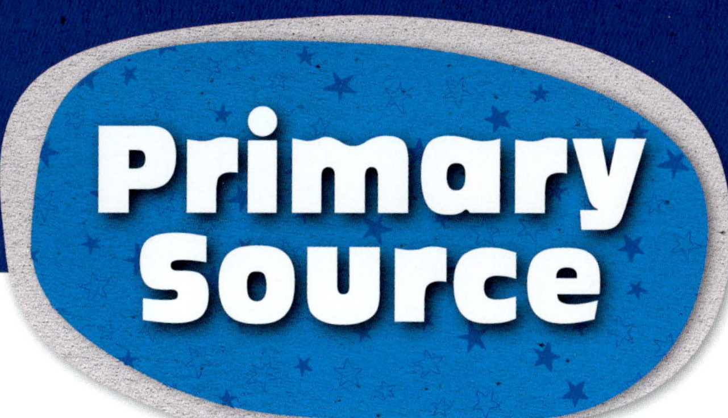

Chef Sean Sherman spoke about Owamni, his restaurant focusing on American Indian foods:

> We look at showcasing the amazing diversity and flavor profiles of all the different tribes across North America . . . and cutting away **Colonial** ingredients. We don't have things on our menu that have dairy, wheat flour, cane sugar, . . . beef, pork, or chicken.

Source: Sam Briger. "The Sioux Chef Uses Only Native Ingredients, but Isn't 'Cooking Like It's 1491.'" *NPR*, 24 Oct. 2022, npr.org. Accessed 8 Aug. 2023.

What's the Big Idea?

What is this quote's main idea? Explain how the main idea is supported by details.

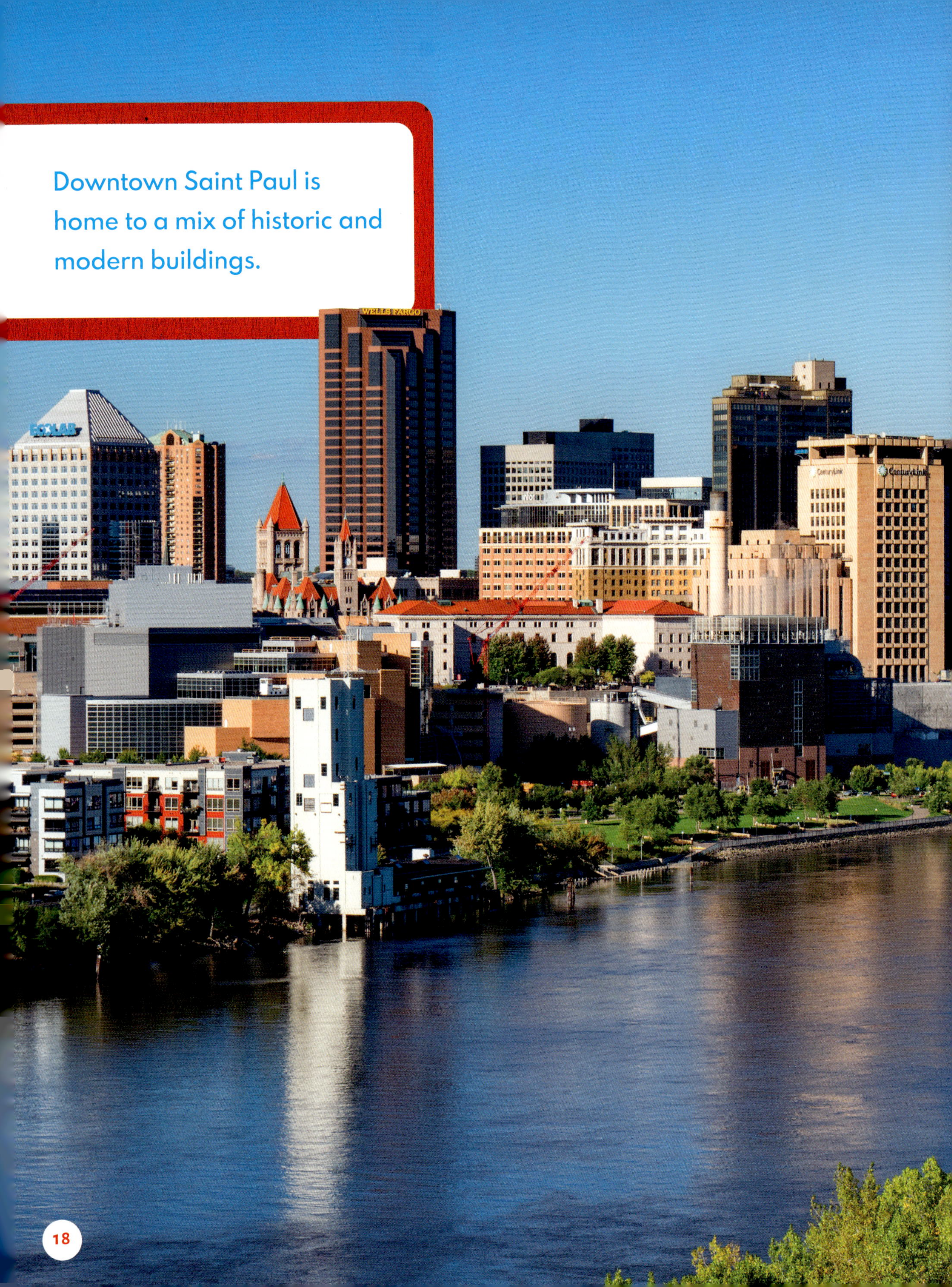

Downtown Saint Paul is home to a mix of historic and modern buildings.

CHAPTER 3

Places in Minnesota

The capital of Minnesota is Saint Paul. It is located along the Mississippi River. The river divides Minneapolis and Saint Paul. Together, these cities are known as the Twin Cities. Most of the state's people live in the Twin Cities and their **suburbs**.

In 2023, Minnesota decided on a new state flag. An eight-point North Star sits in a dark-blue panel shaped like Minnesota. The light blue represents the state's many lakes.

Saint Cloud is in central Minnesota. Rochester is found in the southeast. Duluth is on the shore of Lake Superior. There are several American Indian reservations in Minnesota too. Seven are Anishinaabe, and four are Dakota.

In Duluth, people can watch ships pass under the Duluth Aerial Lift Bridge.

At Gooseberry Falls State Park, visitors can see the Upper, Middle, and Lower Falls of the Gooseberry River.

Parks

Minnesota has one national park. It is called Voyageurs National Park. It is on the state's northern border. The park contains large lakes. Visitors can use canoes to reach campsites.

Minnesota also has 66 state parks and nine recreation areas. The most popular state park is Gooseberry Falls. It is on the shore of Lake Superior. It features hiking trails, beautiful waterfalls, and a visitor center. Itasca is another popular state park. It features the spot where the Mississippi River begins at Lake Itasca.

Landmarks

The meeting place of the Minnesota River and Mississippi River is an important location.

It was a trading site for the Ojibwe. When white settlers arrived, they built Fort Snelling there. Today, this place is an important Minnesota landmark. Visitors can tour historical buildings. They can learn about the site's history.

Another landmark is the Minnesota State Fairgrounds. This area between Minneapolis

The Minnesota State Fair

The Minnesota State Fair is the nation's largest state fair by daily attendance. Visitors can see animals, look at artwork, and go on rides. Attendees can also enjoy concerts and other live entertainment. The State Fair is famous for its many foods and drinks.

The Minnesota State Fair is often called the Great Minnesota Get-Together. The fairgrounds include rides such as the SkyGlider and Ferris wheel.

and Saint Paul is where the Minnesota State Fair is held. The popular gathering happens each year in late summer.

The Cathedral of Saint Paul is about 306 feet (93 m) tall. It has stained glass windows and walls made from Minnesota stone.

The Cathedral of Saint Paul is a famous Saint Paul landmark. This huge Catholic church opened in 1915. The building has a large copper dome. The church can be seen from miles away.

Minnesota has an amazing mix of landscapes and cultures. People can canoe in Voyageurs National Park, visit the State Fair, or shop at the Mall of America. They can taste a variety of dishes and learn about the state's history. The Land of 10,000 Lakes has something for everyone.

Further Evidence

Look at the website below, which contains a map of Minnesota state parks. Does it give any new evidence to support Chapter Three?

Minnesota State Parks and Recreation Areas

abdocorelibrary.com/discovering-minnesota

State Map

Duluth

Saint Paul

KEY

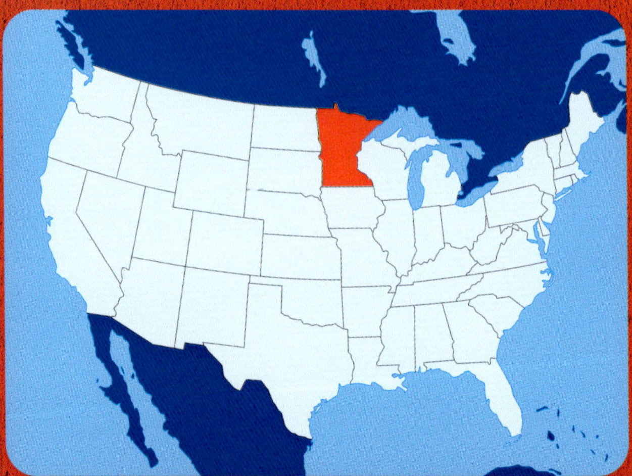

Minnesota: The North Star State
CANADA
Voyageurs
National Park
Bemidji
Gooseberry Falls
State Park
Lake Superior
Mississippi
River
Itasca
State Park
Duluth
North Dakota
Saint
Cloud
Saint Croix
River
Mississippi
River
Saint
Paul
Wisconsin
Minneapolis
South Dakota
Mall of
America
Minnesota River
Minnesota
River
Mississippi River
N
W
E
S
Rochester
Iowa

Glossary

Colonial
related to the 13 British colonies that became the United States, or to the period before they became independent

famine
a severe lack of food

immigrant
a person who moves to a different country

manufacturing
the process of making goods to sell

refugees
people who leave a country to escape danger

rural
relating to the countryside rather than the city

suburbs
the smaller cities next to a larger city

Online Resources

To learn more about Minnesota, visit our free resource websites below.

Visit **abdocorelibrary.com** or scan this QR code for free Common Core resources for teachers and students, including vetted activities, multimedia, and booklinks, for deeper subject comprehension.

Visit **abdobooklinks.com** or scan this QR code for free additional online weblinks for further learning. These links are routinely monitored and updated to provide the most current information available.

Learn More

Lilley, Matt. *Minnesota's Devil's Kettle*. Abdo, 2021.

Murray, Julie. *Minnesota*. Abdo, 2020.

Payne, Stefanie. *The National Parks*. DK, 2020.

Index

Cathedral of Saint Paul, 26

Dakota peoples, 11–12, 20

food, 15, 16, 17, 24
Fort Snelling, 24

Gooseberry Falls State Park, 23

immigrants, 12–13
Itasca State Park, 23

Lake Superior, 8, 20, 23
lakes, 7, 8, 15, 20, 23, 27

Mall of America, 5–7, 9, 27
Mayo Clinic, 16
Minneapolis, 15, 19, 24
Minnesota State Fairgrounds, 24–25, 27
Mississippi River, 8, 19, 23

Ojibwe peoples, 11–12, 24

Saint Paul, 6, 19, 25, 26
Sherman, Sean, 15, 17
state symbols, 6

Voyageurs National Park, 23, 27

About the Author

Arnold Ringstad is a writer and editor. He has lived in Minnesota for more than 30 years.